The Science of Myths
and Vice Versa

The Science of Myths and Vice Versa

Gregory Schrempp

PRICKLY PARADIGM PRESS
CHICAGO

Notes for this pamphlet can be found online in a PDF
at http://www.prickly-paradigm.com/titles.html

Prickly Paradigm Press, LLC
5629 South University Avenue
Chicago, IL 60637

www.prickly-paradigm.com

ISBN: 9780996635509
LCCN: 2016941733

Printed in the United States of America on acid-free paper.

Myth and Science

"Myth" and "science" both occur in numerous hybrid pairings: mythopoeic, mythico-religious; protoscience, pseudoscience, and so on—a propensity that attests equally to the importance and to the fuzziness of these concepts. The essays that follow address an even more problematic hybridism, the one that combines these two polarized terms directly with one another. What should we call it: myth-science? mythico-science? mythoscience? At issue are non-fictional formulations that attempt to blend legitimate contemporary science with characters, scenarios, or patterns that we typically associate with traditional mythologies. A not insignificant part of popular educational literature and television (popular science, but other genres as well, including numerous forms of political and cultural commentary) offers some such blend. These blends form a powerful force in contemporary culture and consciousness, in part because they tap into and align two different sources of authority and persuasion. The analysis that follows will explore and elaborate the blending process through four recent examples.

There are plentiful ways in which such blends of science and mythology can be achieved. The four examples I explore in this analysis share an important characteristic: each is built on a familiar scenario from the past re-appearing in a way that throws into relief the relation between science and mythology. The most radical kind of foregrounding of this relation is displayed in the first and last essays, which consider stories—respectively that of David and Goliath, and that of the domestication of fire for cooking—that first appear in human history as mythology, but more recently have reappeared in the guise of science. Like a wheel within a wheel: the second essay, on Stephen Greenblatt's recent best-selling book *The Swerve*, which deals with the renaissance rediscovery of Lucretius, and the third, on Neil deGrasse Tyson's re-make of Carl Sagan's classic television series *Cosmos*, arise, each in its own way, not so much from mythology turning into science (though this is part of it), but rather from mythologized science turning into re-mythologized science. The two cycles are of vastly different size, Lucretius—in a big cycle with numerous epicycles—coming around again after two millennia, *Cosmos* orbiting back after only thirty-four years.

Having leapt into the complicated issue of mythology and science, I will offer some clarifications on my approach. For present purposes "mythology" and "science," terms often rhetorically invoked as opposites, are approached as fuzzy-set concepts. Like all opposed sets, there is a substrate of unifying characteristics; the most basic is that mythology and science both offer accounts of the workings of nature (hence

Frazer's notion of myth as "protoscience"). Other shared qualities could be added; for example, both involve imagination, are intrigued by the periodicities of nature, and are drawn toward overarching or integrative principles. Regarding the concept of mythology, some of the more recurrent features are narrative exposition (i.e., story-telling), nature portrayed as working through personal forces (animism and anthropomorphism), heroes who lay down moral values and precedents, and some sense of a sacred (over against mundane) reality. Features that, by contrast, distinguish science include logical or argumentative (as opposed to narrative) exposition, a view of nature working through unvarying, impersonal, natural laws (and a concomitant disavowal of animism and anthropomorphism), epistemological materialism, structured experimentation, and methods based on higher-level mathematics and statistics. Following anthropologist/mythologist Claude Lévi-Strauss, my concluding essay will consider yet another other way in which myth and science have been distinguished, namely, that the former operates at the level of the senses, while the latter operates at a level below the senses (e.g., atomic elements or molecules).

Of course any one of these features of myth or science might occasion momentous debate. But rather than entering into such debate, I will ask the reader to press forward with this rough-and-ready approximation to see whether it is not useful in enlightening the topics considered in the four essays that follow.

My examples stem from recent popular culture in the United States, where mythoscience is flourishing —indeed it forms a veritable industry. In my concluding essay, the quest for the origin of cooking is mapped onto a journey from California to North Carolina; and, more broadly, such culinary journeys—"on the road" in search of the perfect diner or pulled-pork—has become a common trope in American regionally-flavored foodie-literature. But it is not as though I think the US has a monopoly on food, the contemporary food-renaissance, stories about journeys or pilgrimages, or for that matter on the desire to fuse the mythic and the scientific. Similarly, regarding the first essay (on David and Goliath), it is clear to me that Americans are obsessed with winning, and it seems that some ways of packaging this theme (for example within ultimately Calvinistic tones of self-help or self-improvement) can impart a "typically American" flavor to the obsession. But I suspect that there is no society that entirely lacks stories about winning (and doing so through cleverness); so this essay is perhaps best seen as dealing with an American variation on a widely-spread if not universal narrative theme.

In an argument that now circulates as an adage, distinguished philosopher of science Karl Popper proposed that "science must begin with myths." The claim epitomizes his view that the essential epistemic dynamic of science lies in the work of falsification. Here is the original context of the statement:

A critical attitude needs for its raw material, as it were, theories or beliefs which are held more or less dogmatically.

Thus science must begin with myths, and with the criticism of myths; neither with the collection of observations, nor with the invention of experiments, but with the critical discussion of myths, and of magical techniques and practices. The scientific tradition is distinguished from the pre-scientific tradition in having two layers. Like the latter, it passes on its theories; but it also passes on a critical attitude towards them. The theories are passed on, not as dogmas, but rather with the challenge to discuss them and improve upon them.

The examples I discuss in the following essays do reflect, though ambivalently in at least one case, the imperative that Popper lays out in this statement: science improves upon teachings that for some at least have been matters of dogma or received wisdom. But in these same examples one also senses two other imperatives that are not adequately represented in Popper's portrayal of the relation of myth and science. One is love of myth and hence the desire, even if unexplicated or unconscious, to preserve it as a thing of value in itself; this process is explored in the classical and medieval world by Luc Brisson in his *How Philosophers Saved Myths.* Analogously, in the modern world of science the consummate, unsentimental scientist may be ready to dispense with the original in favor of the improvement, but, especially for a popular audience, the prospect of retaining both may be more appealing.

The other imperative lies in the fact that there are cases in which the *reverse* of Popper's dictum is appropriate: mythology begins in science. Obvious examples are Sagan's and Tyson's *Cosmos* series, which take findings of modern science and spin them into new, enticing humanistic visions full of adventure, spectacle, and moral rumination. But there is also a broader problem with locating science, as per Popper's comment, entirely in a second, superadded layer of intellection, for doing so leaves the first layer bereft of anything like a critical spirit. True, a formalized critical dialectic is not generally part of what we term mythology, but neither is mythology indifferent to empirical reality and a sense of accountability towards it. For all that we now find problematic in Frazer's attitudes towards myth and science, he was wise in not drawing an absolute line between them.

1
David and Goliath: The Rematch

In the biblical book of Samuel we encounter a story pivotal to the history of ancient Israel, recounting a startling event that marks the beginning of the ascension of David as king. As the Philistines encroach on the Kingdom of Israel though the Valley of Elah, one of their warriors, named Goliath, issues a challenge that the battle be decided by combat between himself and any warrior that Israel chooses to put up against him. Goliath is of imposing dimensions; none of the Israelites steps up until finally David, a small, young shepherd boy from Bethlehem, accepts. With no other prospect, King Saul allows David to go up against Goliath, and David, armorless and with only a sling and five stones, achieves a surprising victory, at which the Philistines flee.

In his 2013 book *David and Goliath: Underdogs, Misfits, and the Art of Battling Giants*, Malcolm Gladwell has approached this biblical story through methods and perspectives drawn from modern science, to offer a surprising new interpretation of the events recounted. I will examine Gladwell's new reading after first considering two earlier readings, the first a pre-Gladwellian traditional religious reading, the second an "intermediate" reading that, like Gladwell's, brings in modern science—but only so far.

A Pre-Gladwellian Religious Reading

I will call my first reading naïve or trusting, both because it takes the propositions making up the biblical narrative pretty much at face value, and in the sense that it is essentially the story as I learned and understood it in (religiously "pre-critical") early grade-school Bible class. In this reading, the story is about the power of divine providence as embraced and implemented through the religiously-infused courage of a particular individual. Everything relating to Goliath is massive and fearsome; everything pertaining to David is small, light, and unthreatening (epitomized in the five smooth stones from a creek bed). David possesses a steadfast confidence in the providence of the Lord, as expressed in one of the most fervent biblical testimonials, addressed first to Saul and then to Goliath: "The Lord that delivered me out of the paw of the lion, and out of the paw of the bear, he will deliver me out of the hand of this Philistine."

David's success derives from his personal right-eousness and courage coupled to the favor of the Lord towards his steadfast servants and, more deeply, toward the nation of Israel via a covenant made with Abraham and recounted in the book of Exodus: "And I will take you to me for a people, and I will be to you a God."

The very improbability of the victory attests to the courage and steadfastness of David and the power and providence of the Lord toward his chosen people. In Bible class, this is what I understood the story of David and Goliath to be about, and I suspect that such an understanding is similar to that of many individuals, past and present, who learned the story in a religious context, or, if learning it in a non-religious context, understood it to be a religious story.

An Intermediate Reading

Before turning to Gladwell's reading, I will briefly comment on an "intermediate" reading, one which lies between the pre-Gladwellian, religious reading offered above, and Gladwell's thoroughly scientific reading. The exemplary figure for the intermediate reading is James Frazer, whose *Folklore in the Old Testament* examines stories, themes, and motifs from scriptural texts of Judaism and Christianity and systematically reveals parallels in surrounding mythico-religious traditions. Frazer's method was an attempt to be scientifically objective through a comparative method as opposed to adhering to the authority of a single cultural tradition.

Unlike some of the Old Testament stories he examines (including his especially notorious analysis of the story of the "Fall of Man" in Eden), Frazer makes only one point about the story of David and Goliath, specifically that David is the youngest of a set of brothers. As knowledgeable as Frazer was on world oral narratives, he could have gone much further, and it is surprising that he did not. For from Maui the Polynesian demi-god and trickster, to Zeus contra

Cronus (and in turn Cronus contra Uranus), to folktale heroine Cinderella, world oral narrative favors the scenario of a younger sibling triumphing over older. Another conceit common in world mythology is the exaggeration of physical dimensions and characteristics of principals; and here David and Goliath fall right in line. Temporal units are often ritualized in culturally specific ways—or is it just a coincidence that Goliath is said to have hurled his challenge for the same period of 40 days that rain poured down on Noah? The idea of battles fought by a single individual representing each side does occur often in ancient literature, but typically in contexts distant enough that it would be difficult to find verification, raising the possibility that this too might be a concession to narrative drama. Finally and most importantly, the world of traditional fables is full of stories of victories by underdogs whose virtues are underestimated in the face of apparent superiority, whether in terms of speed (The Tortoise and the Hare) or size (The Lion and the Mouse). The story of David and Goliath possibly first arose as a sort of historicized and theologized fable; but at any rate we will see that Gladwell, not the first to do so, goes in the other direction, turning the story of a nominally historical event into a fable by extracting a bit of paradigmatic practical wisdom: "There is an important lesson...for battles with all kinds of giants. The powerful and the strong are not always what they seem."

As noted above, the Frazerian style of analysis does not alter the logic of the story, but rather attempts to put that logic into world context. The overall effect is to raise doubts about the uniqueness or specialness of the Judaeo-Christian, or any other, religious tradition. While the comparative anthropological "science" of mythology/religion induces skepticism—for some religious people creating doubts greater than those precipitated by any of the physical sciences—the ushering of science into mythology in the Frazerian manner does not involve probing very deeply into the analysis of the narrated events themselves.

What is the relation of Gladwell's project to Frazer's? Like Frazer, Gladwell incorporates the spirit of science into the interpretation of mythology, but he does so more radically, drawing on science to offer a reinterpretation of *what happened* at the Valley of Elah.

Gladwell's Reading

Malcolm Gladwell is a prolific, best-selling author, a contemporary public guru "masterful at explaining how the world works" (Lionel Beehner in *USA Today* as quoted on the cover of *David and Goliath*). He focuses on scenarios drawn from or relevant to contemporary society—economy, technology, and sports, for example—to offer novel takes on seemingly straightforward scenarios, many already familiar to his readers. His writing is a mixture of popular science (including popular cognitive science) and cultural analysis, and blends easily into the realms of motivational speaking and self-help. Each chapter of *David and Goliath* "tells the story of a different person—famous or unknown, ordinary or brilliant—who has faced an outsize challenge and been forced to respond."

Gladwell is insistent that all along "we've been telling these kinds of stories wrong. *David and Goliath* is about getting them right." Our understanding is deficient because we have regarded the victory of the underdog as miraculous and "improbable." In a TED-talk version of the scenario, Gladwell is more personal: "everything I thought I knew about that story turned out to be wrong." Gladwell's new reading culminates in the claim that the seemingly improbable outcome is actually the probable one.

The new factors, absent (at least with any analytical explicitness) from the biblical story and introduced to the scenario of David and Goliath by Gladwell, derive from three different branches of contemporary science and technology.

The first set of factors derives from ballistic and military-strategy analysis, for which Gladwell cites several experts. Via an analysis of the projectile's speed we learn that that David's sling would have carried the stopping power of a modern handgun. In the TED-talk version Gladwell adds that the stones of the area would have been made of barium sulphate, with twice the density of normal stones. Gladwell presents David's strategy as new, unconventional, and sophisticated as opposed to the encumbered and outdated mode of warfare epitomized by Goliath.

The second type of factor derives from the science of medicine, in particular from historical pathology and forensics—fields that recently have captured public imagination in numerous contemporary television dramas (e.g., *NCIS*, *Bones*, *Cold Case*). Gladwell cites a tradition of medical experts speculating that Goliath suffered from a condition known as acromegaly that is produced by a pituitary tumor, effects of which include gigantism and impaired movement and vision.

The hints of disease adduced by Gladwell from the biblical text are intriguing, but it must be said that all of these elements could be explained just as convincingly in terms of the contributions they make to the poetic power of the narrative. For example, that Goliath was preceded by a shield-bearer Gladwell explains as indicating impaired vision (Goliath had to be led), but this motif is as easily relatable to the psychological allure of military pageantry, omnipresent in ancient epics, and the fable-like contrast between mass (an already massive Goliath with even more weight to be added once he takes up his shield) and the small, self-contained, lithe David whose armament fit in his shepherd's pouch. The contrast is heightened by the very occupations of the combatants—warrior vs. protector (i.e., shepherd).

The third set of scientific elements derives from outside the story and even the larger Judaic scriptural corpus. For, like Frazer, Gladwell puts the David and Goliath battle in world-comparative context—only this time the object of comparison is not mythological motifs but rather the outcomes, statistically calculated, of battles fought between large and small forces. Here Gladwell cites analyses by political scientist Ivan Arreguín-Toft that claim to show that in battles between larger and smaller forces, in which the smaller force uses "unconventional or guerrilla tactics," the smaller force wins 63.6 % of the time. Or, as Gladwell simplifies, "Underdogs win all the time." The victory that we have been misunderstanding as improbable is revealed, via statistical analysis, to be the probable outcome; in this refigured rematch, David thus wins again, but for updated reasons. Statistical analysis reappears in many forms through Gladwell's book as he ranges through a variety of upset victories, from personal to political, concluding with the defeat of the giant in Vietnam.

However, the issue of whether pre-Gladwellian readers see David's victory as improbable is more complicated than Gladwell allows. I submit that in the pre-Gladwellian and Gladwellian accounts the probable and improbable stand in a precisely parallel relationship. In both readings the story is propelled by a tension between a surface analysis that points to improbability and a deeper metaphysics that points to probability. In both cases, an apparently unlikely outcome is rendered probable by a particular community's recognition of a more esoteric causality beneath or beyond the surface of things. Both versions are about personal courage and strategy, but linked to and backed by another force. In one case the other force is the causality of *divine providence* sealed in a Covenant (which is repeatedly and unmistakably indexed in the biblical story, whether or not any particular hearer or reader believes in it); in the other, it is the equally mysterious but impersonal force or principles—or whatever it is—that eventuates in *statistical probabilities*. Both readings offer metaphysical assurance of an "improbable" victory via a deeper reality which, so to speak, only a philistine would fail to grasp. Gladwell is only one of several contemporary writers who tap the quirks of statistical analysis to offer an inspiring message—a message of hope to those who feel powerless; another, even more recent example is David J. Hand's *The Improbability Principle: Why Coincidences, Miracles, and Rare Events Happen Every Day* (2014).

The theme of divine causation is present in Gladwell's *David and Goliath*, but in the form of a reporting of David's beliefs rather than Gladwell himself endorsing those beliefs within his analysis. Gladwell quotes part of David's religious testimonial when facing Goliath and characterizes David as going into battle "powered by courage and faith." The latter comment might reasonably be taken as suggesting that

Gladwell sees David's religiously based confidence as contributing to his success, but other than this Gladwell offers neither rejection nor endorsement of the principle of divine influence actually operating in the world. The world that Gladwell's analysis in *David and Goliath* does index is, rather, the world of contemporary popular science, self-help, motivational speaking, and TED-talks. This is a world whose repeating themes, secular but often inflected in spiritual and visionary tones, include fascination with science and technology coupled with the conviction that these have bequeathed the possibility for new understanding of the world and momentous personal and social transformation; the need for innovative, out-of-the-box thinking, and for agility and adaptability amidst astoundingly rapid change; the power of underdogs (and small, nimble startups) as heroes going against powerful but slow-moving, heartless, amoral, outmoded institutions and ideas (dinosaurs, Goliaths); the creative outflow spawned by unconventional individuals and by cultural diversity and global interchange; and, most of all, the need for rules of ultimate wisdom for understanding the world, taking control, winning, and feeling good about oneself amidst all of this. When Gladwell charges that we have been misunderstanding the story of David and Goliath and now must set about getting it right, surely he means *right for this worldview.*

Whatever Gladwell's own views on the matter, no doubt at least some of his readers will find ways of reconciling the pre- and post-Gladwellian readings, thereby not only reconciling God and Science but receiving a double assurance of improbable victory. Religious apologists will say that the biblical "days" of creation really means evolutionary "epochs" and the plague of the Nile River turning to blood is a religious dramatization of an outbreak of micro-organic dinoflagellates. Attempts to rationalize the miraculous elements of mythology are part of a broader stream in the interpretation of mythology which, for religious, political, and other reasons, has been part of western intellectual history at least since Livy's history of Rome. Enlightenment philosophers sometimes proposed that the Divine Mind is identical with the laws of nature, so there can be no final conflict between God and Mathematics. A modern cognitive-science perspective might regard religious thought as an adaptive mechanism for intuitively and unconsciously synthesizing useful strategies that will later be borne out by science.

God works in mysterious ways (by placing barium sulfate under David's feat and by afflicting Goliath with acromegaly?). A more practical reconciliation (associated with the "protestant ethic" and the Norman Vincent Peale style of religiously-infused strategies for success, a precursor of contemporary self-help literature) is that "God helps those who help themselves"—or, in present parlance, those with a good business plan. Peale and his associate, psychiatrist Smiley Blanton, sometimes boosted the appeal of their work by combining the authority of religion and science. For example, one edition of their joint-authored book *Faith is the Answer* bears the subtitle *A Psychiatrist and A Pastor Discuss Your Problems*, while another edition bears the prominent front-cover message, "NEW enlarged edition of the famous book uniting two great sciences—Faith and Psychology—to offer satisfying answers to the many problems of everyday living." Additionally, human psychology is complex and functionally flexible; there are no doubt individuals who will think of David and Goliath at one moment as a story about divine providence and at another as about ballistics and statistics.

Still, there is a limit to the fusability of the two readings and their respective metaphysics—a limit revealed especially when one tries to combine the two readings into a unified David and Goliath proposition. One then ends up with a scenario less coherent and edifying than either reading furnishes alone, if not one that is downright unedifying, something like: statistically, a courageous and devout small combatant favored by the Lord and armed with superior ballistics and unconventional strategy will overcome a large combatant impaired by a brain tumor. Sometimes it is better just to stick with one version or the other.

2
Lucretius Swerves Back Around

Lucretius was a first-century BCE Roman poet who, in his epic poem *De Rerum Natura*, championed the materialistic, atomistic worldview of the fourth/third-century BCE Greek philosopher Epicurus. The central theme of Lucretius' poem is that acceptance of materialistic atomism over the teachings of religion and mythology will promote happiness and tranquility by displacing the great sources of human anxiety, especially fear of death. Lucretius heroizes Epicurus, and the readers who will follow him, through a metaphorical sea journey from dark and stormy waters to a sunlit and tranquil harbor. Like other epics of the time, the journey is punctuated by evocations of perils and mythological gods and images, leading some contemporary scholars to wonder about the heavy dose of mythology in a work that aims to dislodge the cosmic picture portrayed in mythology. A likely possibility is that Lucretius is following in the footsteps of Plato (specifically the model of the Allegory of the Cave) in offering an anti-myth myth, that is, tapping mythological imagery—most obvious in the transition from darkness to light—to dramatize the possibility of humanity moving to an understanding of the cosmos superior to that offered by mythology. At many points Lucretius invokes mythology to provoke a show-down. This is most evident in the "transit of Venus" that occurs between Book 1 (which opens with a salute to Venus as the source of the regenerative power of nature) and Book 4 (in which the goddess is dismissed and denounced as emblem of the desires that derail the tranquil spirit), the books in-between serving to introduce an alternative account of nature's powers: the theory of atomism. Many contemporary popular science writers also follow some such strategy.

Greenblatt's Lucretius

In his 2011 book *The Swerve: How the World Became Modern*, Stephen Greenblatt, a literary scholar specializing in the Renaissance, pulled a best-seller out of a topic of the sort generally confined to the ivory tower: the fifteenth-century rediscovery of Lucretius. Greenblatt's success has been attributed to many of the usual novelistic factors: accessibility, interesting characters, rapid pace, and, most of all, page-turning suspense as the key that opens the Renaissance, *De Rerum Natura*, is rescued from oblivion through a chance rediscovery by an eccentric genius and book-hunter. But underlying these factors is something else. I will argue that Greenblatt infuses Lucretius with a mythic appeal that, despite many differences, is at base very much like that which Lucretius supplies for Epicurus;

in other words, Greenblatt is to Lucretius as Lucretius is to Epicurus. Like Lucretius, Greenblatt is a hero-mythologizer, a claim I will elaborate through three aspects of myth: narrative structure, the character of the hero (this will not be about Joseph Campbell), and engagement of micro-/macrocosm play that is typical in mythology.

Mythic Narrative Structure

Lucretius and Greenblatt frame their respective hero stories mythically—though I suspect this is done with more conscious literary strategy by Lucretius than by Greenblatt, whose mythologizing gestures may arise, predictably if unconsciously, as a byproduct of the awe he holds for Lucretius and the historical place he has reserved for him. More specifically, the frame adopted by both Lucretius and Greenblatt is that of a *transformation* myth, a type of origin myth described by scholars of mythology, Franz Boas among them, as contrasting with the frame of *creation* myths. In *creation* myths, the cosmos actually comes into being. In *transformation* myths, the cosmos is assumed to have always been (or at least its origin is not made a matter of concern); then at some point, as a result of a culture hero and actions that if not miraculous are at least beyond the ordinary, the cosmos undergoes a shift that makes it suitable for human life. In transformation myths, there are just these two cosmic epochs: unsuitable for humanity, and suitable. Lucretius in effect presents Epicurus as the culture hero who made possible the transition from stormy sea to sunlit harbor; while Greenblatt presents the 15th century re-discovery of *De Rerum Natura* by book-hunter Poggio Bracciolini—a stand-in hero for

Lucretius—as precipitant of the "change from one way of perceiving and living in the world to another." The "swerve," which in Epicurus and Lucretius is an argument about a quirk in the movement of atoms that gives rise to free will, becomes for Greenblatt a metaphor for a course-change in human history: not a creation from nothing, but a fundamental transformation in how life is to be lived. Greenblatt concludes his Preface by furthering the birth metaphor—given in the term "renaissance," but also one of the world's favorite idioms of cosmogonic origin—to describe Poggio's role: "The act of discovery fulfilled the life's passion of a brilliant book hunter. And that book hunter, without ever intending or realizing it, became a midwife to modernity." The recovery of Lucretius "permanently changed the landscape of the world." It is worth noting that in traditional mythologies transformer-heroes typically do not see themselves as such; they act to satisfy some intense, immediate impulse, not with designs on changing the world.

The dramatic, all-encompassing transformation from dark to light via a culture hero is made clear by Lucretius, in repeated paeans like this one:

> When human life lay groveling in all men's sight, crushed to the earth under the dead weight of superstition…, a man of Greece [Epicurus] was first to raise mortal eyes in defiance, first to stand erect and brave the challenge. Fables of the gods did not crush him, nor the lightning flash and the growling menace of the sky.

Admittedly we find nothing quite this melodramatic regarding Lucretius in Greenblatt. Indeed a fair bit of the opening to *The Swerve* goes in the opposite direction, voicing tendencies of modern historiographic sensibility that temper the quest for heroes and sudden, all-encompassing changeovers. The most important is an insistence that the larger intellectual context of any idea or event be considered; if I am not mistaken a rather standard consequence of careful, multi-source historiography is to blunt purported "revolutions" and "revolutionaries" with the discovery of multiple thinkers building on one-another's ideas—ideas in circulation, in other words—and with a view of change as flowing from a tangle of interacting and accumulating factors. This tendency can temper the notion of "hero" in yet another way: by emphasizing the momentum that flows from the lesser-knowns—and, at some point, the anonymous bearers of everyday habits of thought and practice—that make up the culture, or emergent culture, of a particular time and place.

What is striking in Greenblatt is the extent to which, despite the influence of such historiographic sensibilities, a mytho-cosmogonic drama of dark and light still seeps to the surface. Greenblatt notes that there have been numerous "forgettings" and "recoveries" and that there is no "vivid symbol"—no "fall of the Bastille"—associated with the story he is telling, only the discovery of an old manuscript in a library. But then he adds, in a theme that will be repeated several times through the narrative, that "if he [Poggio] had had an intimation of the forces he was unleashing, he might have thought twice about drawing so explosive a work out of the darkness in which it slept." Given Greenblatt's historiographic allegiances and his audience, this is about as close to a culture hero/transformation myth as he can get away with (or almost so:

one of the criticisms of *The Swerve* is the over-enthusiastic dichotomizing). The cautions are easily forgotten while engaging the narrative of Poggio's cliff-hanger discovery of the now twice-born Lucretius. This narrative of Poggio, which forms the inner, and larger, part of Greenblatt's book, amounts to a sort of detective story resonating as a cultural origin myth. By championing Poggio, Greenblatt does in a way honor the unknowns and minor players of history; and yet Poggio's near anonymity for our era (prior to Greenblatt's book) ends up as a device for dramatizing the magnitude of his role.

The Mythic Hero

The Swerve is not short on cosmically pivotal figures. In the course of the narrative of Poggio's book-hunting, Greenblatt says that Lucretius viewed Epicurus as a "saviour," a "hero," and a "messiah"; that Virgil saw Lucretius as a "culture hero"; and that Poggio's friends saw Poggio himself as a "culture hero." Greenblatt appears to share such sentiments toward the three, who in a way converge into one mythic figure. Mythologists employ the term *culture hero* to designate those heroes who first bring culture to humans—culture in the sense of some form of knowledge, technology, or rule that defines a distinctively human way of life. Humanity is envisioned by contrast with animality, and/or the barbarism of other peoples, and/or a group's mythically projected view of its own "savagery" prior to acquiring its most valuable possession(s) and life-ways. Culture heroes break time into two epochs, creating a humanly defining before and after. (As we will consider in the final essay, Lévi-

Strauss regards fire as the quintessential culture-hero gift, one that ushers in others.) For Lucretius, the human boon is the epicurean life; for Greenblatt, it is Lucretius' rendition of the epicurean spirit writ large as the Renaissance.

Both Lucretius and Greenblatt are also what I will call the hero-herald: not the hero themselves, but the figure who points out, or points to, the hero. Some hero-heralds are precursors (such as John the Baptist for Jesus) while others point backwards in time—but also forward with respect to the audience they hope to influence—to a hero whom some of us may have missed (e.g., Plato for Socrates, Dawkins for Darwin). Heroes and their heralds generally hail from the same discipline or way of life (both are religious teachers, or both are scientists, and so on). This is so for Greenblatt and Lucretius, with an intriguing twist: both are crossovers, that is, literary/artistic figures who nevertheless credit a new teaching about *physical matter* with allowing human life and culture to shift in substantial and beneficial ways: from groveling to flourishing—thus, one might add, making the world safe for art and artists.

In Greenblatt, the move suggests an interesting parallel with, and contrast to, the transformation myths of contemporary popular science writers, who similarly attribute the possibility of moral and epistemological uplift to a shift in the picture of the physical cosmos that took place a half millennium ago. But popular science writers most often choose Copernicus (virtually never Lucretius) as the pivotal figure who, in an act of cosmo-paradigmatic course-correction, ended our long floundering in darkness and self-deception—at least for those willing to follow. Scholars generally choose heroes who parallel their own occupations.

Greenblatt cursorily mentions Copernicus (whose work was published in the century following the rebirth of Lucretius), treating Copernicus's "intellectual daring" not as the pivotal point but rather as part of a larger intellectual/cultural energy that had already been unleashed. Contemporary popular science writers generally strive to add some sort of aesthetic appeal to their expositions of science; the end result often has the feel of an artistic coating. For Greenblatt, a literary scholar rather than a scientist, the relation between art and science (in the sense of teachings about physical matter) is more complex and clearly bi-directional: on one hand, a new physical teaching dispels ignorance and frees art; on the other, modern science emerges as an emanation of the spirit of renaissance art, which "epitomized the Lucretian embrace of beauty and pleasure" and "suffused" the scientific work of Leonardo da Vinci, Galileo, and Francis Bacon among others.

One other mythic hero pattern should be noted: the motif of the momentous event that almost doesn't happen. This motif (or its popular culture inversion: the time-bomb defused with one second remaining) is common enough that one could not use its presence to label something a myth. Still, there is undoubtedly some form of attraction between culture heroes and the just-barely-happened theme, perhaps arising from the philosophical pathos of resting the cosmically momentous on the humanly tenuous and contingent. Maui the Polynesian trickster harnesses cosmic fire by almost extinguishing all fire, the final remnant escaping into a tree from which it can still be extracted through friction—so we can make fire, but just barely. The so-called totemic-animal "earth-divers" of Native American mythology succeed in establishing land amidst the expanse of water when the last of them to try almost expires in bringing up a tiny paw-ful of earth from the bottom of the sea. And then there is Poggio's rescue of the manuscript, on the verge of eternal loss, without which the renaissance would be, minimally, diluted and delayed: "Apart from a few odds and ends and secondhand reports, all that was left of the whole rich tradition was contained in that single work. A random fire, an act of vandalism, a decision to snuff out the last trace of views judged to be heretical, and the course of modernity would have been different." And not just modernity in the abstract, for the concluding paragraph of *The Swerve* brings us to the edge of Malinowskian myth-as-charter or, more specifically, the origin myth of the United States. Greenblatt closes with Thomas Jefferson's epicurean leanings and the American ideal of "the pursuit of Happiness": "The atoms of Lucretius had left their traces on the Declaration of Independence."

Micro-macrocosmic Play

Greenblatt's work is full of temporal themes and relations, a point visible even in the chapter titles (e.g., "The Teeth of Time," "Birth and Rebirth," "The Return," "Afterlives"). Many of the themes are cyclical, encouraging a mythological treatment of Greenblatt under the hackneyed but not unfounded notion that myth has a peculiar slant toward cyclical over lineal time. The temporal macro-referent is the two-millennia-long drama of the birth of the Renaissance: from Greek thinker Epicurus, promoted by Roman epic poet Lucretius, resurrected through a chance rediscovery that stimulated the Renaissance—an event in turn revisited and popularized a few years ago by Greenblatt.

At issue here is not the temporal macro-structure *per se*, but rather the fact, true of culture hero myths generally, that themes in the macro-structure recur in microcosm at the level of the individual believer. In *De Rerum Natura*, Lucretius portrays the journey from darkness to light simultaneously on three levels: the history of humanity, the journey of Epicurus (who "voyaged in mind throughout infinity"), and the education of the reader, for whom *De Rerum Natura* offers a kind of self-help course in epicurean philosophy. Analogously, the "swerve" for Greenblatt is a tiered metaphor, spanning from the micro-movement of atoms—the condition for the possibility of human will—to the macro-movement of human history ("the world swerved in a new direction"), with transformative events in individual lives mediating between the two. Contemporary popular science writers similarly present *their* hero, Copernicus, not just as the emblem of a momentous historical changeover, but as the core symbol in a rite of passage—a sort of ritual of humiliation in which we renounce the claim to be the center of the universe—that all readers who want to become scientific must personally undergo.

That Greenblatt's scholarly life is devoted to the Renaissance is clear, but there are more personal factors as well. In the opening pages Greenblatt tells us that his mother was consumed by fear of death, an anxiety with "manipulative and cruel" consequences; hence Lucretius spoke to a deep point of pain in his own life. Adumbrating the story of Poggio, the "brilliant book hunter" whose chance discovery was midwife to the Renaissance, the opening passage of *The Swerve* is about Greenblatt's chance discovery, while a student, of a book with an "odd paperback cover" that turned out to be *De Rerum Natura*: "Hidden behind the worldview I recognize as my own is an ancient poem, a poem once lost, apparently irrevocably, and then found."

All of the parallels noted above find summation in a sort of hypothetical/counterfactual rhetoric of the miraculous that surfaces for the great transformation in both *De Rerum Natura* and *The Swerve*, revealing a convergence of voice between ancient epic poem and modern novelistic best-seller. Consider this passage in Greenblatt:

> Of all the ancient masterpieces, this poem is one that should certainly have disappeared, finally and forever, in the company of the lost works that had inspired it. That it did not disappear, that it surfaced after many centuries and began once again to prop-agate its deeply subversive theses, is something one could be tempted to call a miracle. But the author of the poem in question did not believe in miracles.

A similar tone is found also in Lucretius, most robustly in an encomium for Epicurus that opens Book Five. The encomium concludes:

> Ceres, it is said, taught men to use cereals, and Bacchus the imbibing of the vine-grown liquid; yet without these things we could go on living, as we are told that some tribes live even now. But life could not be well lived till our breasts were swept clean. Therefore that man [Epicurus] has a better claim to be called a god whose gospel...is even now bringing soothing solace to the minds of men.

Lucretius' encomium does not say that Epicurus is a god; it says, rather, that if gods (as humans imagine them) really did exist, Epicurus would have to be placed first among them. In sum, both Greenblatt and Lucretius arrive at a rhetoric that opens a subjunctive space for mythical musing within the new physical reality—a rhetoric which says: there are no miracles, but if there were this would be one.

3
Cosmos: The Structure of Mythoscientific Makeovers

The mid 1960s saw a new term—*paradigm*—enter household parlance and take on a life of its own via the ripple-effect of a scholarly book—an event about as common as mass extinction by asteroid. In his controversial *The Structure of Scientific Revolutions*, Thomas Kuhn proposed a recurrent, generalizable process through which paradigm change occurs in science. Kuhn explicates such change through the notions of "normal science" and paradigm "crisis." The former refers to uneventful "puzzle-solving" that goes on within, confirms, and fills out a paradigm without challenging it; while the latter refers to the condition in which anomalies create doubts about the adequacy of the paradigm itself—precipitating ingenious defenses of it and/or defections to other paradigms.

Amidst much fanfare in 2014, Neil deGrasse Tyson hosted a complete remake of Carl Sagan's famed 1980 television series *Cosmos* (Sagan's was subtitled *A*

Personal Voyage, Tyson's *A Spacetime Odyssey*). Is this a Kuhnian "revolution"? With Kuhn's formulations as sounding board, I will here offer some provisional thoughts about processes through which mythoscience (in contrast to science) develops and changes. Vis-à-vis Kuhn, the makeover of *Cosmos* offers its own kind of anomaly: a case in which *makeover is necessary precisely to perpetuate a paradigm.* Kuhn looks backward through the history of science; I am looking into the future, as developments in media technology rapidly relegate old classics to the primitive and the boring even while opening up new possibilities for spectacular remakes.

In one of the most intriguing cosmological formulations of Western cosmology, Immanuel Kant, in the second half of the *Critique of Pure Reason* (the "transcendental dialectic"), depicts cosmological thought as invariably leading into irresolvable antinomies—for example between the bounded and the unbounded, and between the causation of natural law and that of agentive will. In his early article "The Study of Geography" (1887), Franz Boas summarizes the nineteenth-century epistemological dualism of physical vs. moral or historical sciences: "While physical science arises from the logical and aesthetic demands of the human mind, cosmography has its source in the personal feeling of man towards the world, towards the phenomena surrounding him." The legacy of such conflicts is by now evident in the term *cosmos* itself. For present purposes it is necessary to distinguish internal competing valences between what I will call cosmos$_1$ and cosmos$_2$. Cosmos$_2$, the historically later formulation, will here refer to the term as it is typically encountered in modern science, to mean the totality of the universe as a physical entity and natural system. Cosmos$_1$ stems from an older tradition, one from which we may never break free, in which cosmos means something like the humanized universe or a humanizable part of the universe, which is sometimes set off, in traditional mythologies, against a surrounding chaos. More simply, cosmos$_1$ means the mythologized universe, the universe insofar as we envision it as our home. Mythologized does not mean scientifically false, for any description of the physical cosmos$_2$—prescientific or scientific—is incomplete and full of uncertainty about our place, and thus susceptible to a mythologizing (cosmos$_1$) process; that process, I will argue, is the locus of Tyson's *Cosmos* remake.

Put differently, the reason that Kuhn's formulations do not entirely fit Tyson's makeover of *Cosmos* is that Kuhn takes aim at changes in our understanding of the cosmos$_2$, while what Tyson sets out to change is (mostly) a cosmos$_1$. To be sure, cosmos$_1$ and cosmos$_2$ are both implicated in both Kuhn's revolutions and Tyson's makeover, but these diverge in the nature of the relationship. For Kuhn the propulsive force of scientific revolutions arises in theories about the physical structure of the cosmos$_2$—most "paradigmatically" in the question of whether the sun revolves around the earth, or the other way around. But while there is very little in Kuhn's book about mythology in the usual place one looks for it—religion—Kuhn is famous, or infamous, for closely connecting "paradigm" to a concept that is often associated with religion, namely "community." Paradigm implies, for Kuhn, a group of researchers socialized into shared convictions, values, examples, and practices around a particular way of understanding the natural world. The "community" here is a specialized one made up of scientists, and stability and change in this community flow from arguments about the cosmos$_2$. By contrast, in the Tyson remake, changes in the cosmos$_2$ are relatively minor and incidental, and the propulsive force behind the remake is located (mostly) in the cosmos$_1$—a point that I will expand on below.

There is one sense in which both Sagan's and Tyson's *Cosmos* series are entangled in conflicting paradigms and deep social fissure. But this is not at the level at which different scientific paradigms come into conflict. It is rather at the level at which science as a general paradigm of understanding comes up against the kind of religious paradigm that would restrict the role of science in our self-definition. Episodes of public resistance to Sagan's and Tyson's *Cosmos* for the most part have not been about Sagan vs. Tyson but Sagan and/or Tyson vs. conservative religion. Both Sagan and Tyson are quite open in voicing the need to publicly proselytize for the cause of science on this level.

The remake of Sagan's cosmos came about largely through the efforts of three individuals: Ann Druyan, widow of the late Carl Sagan; Neil deGrasse Tyson, the show's host; and Seth MacFarlane, creator of the television series *Family Guy*. These three all participated in a number of interviews and, as is typically the case for celebrities engaging in numerous interviews on the same topic, each developed a set of predictable spiels. Based on scores of interviews and other web-postings, here are, according to Tyson (with some comments echoed by the other principals), the main reasons for the *Cosmos* remake:

- The audience has changed (sometimes expressed as a "new generation" of viewers)

- Film techniques have changed (in particular the catalog of possible "effects" is vastly expanded)

- The science has changed (for example, we now recognize many more planets and moons in the cosmos)

- The social-cultural context has changed (repeatedly mentioned is what one might term a season change: from the *cold war* and *nuclear winter* anxieties associated with Sagan to current anxieties about *global warming*)

- Television viewing has changed (with notes of defensiveness the interviewees assert that the switch from PBS, which produced Sagan's *Cosmos*, to FOX, which did Tyson's, will allow the series to reach an expanded audience)

- Public interest in science is lagging and in need of rejuvenation; moreover, we are in a period of social and economic decline, while other countries are innovating

Of particular note is the fact that of these reasons, just one—that the science has changed—is singled out in interviews as NOT the main motive behind the remake. For example, consider this comment by Tyson:

> I want to clarify that the goal of this *Cosmos* is not to update the science. A lot of science has happened in the last 35 years. We've discovered a thousand exoplanets, for example. But that's not the goal.... *Cosmos* has, as its mission statement, the effort to convey to you why science matters.

This is tantamount to a denial of a Khunian paradigm change. To put it another way, the *Cosmos* makeover was *not* precipitated within cosmology$_2$, the locus of Kuhnian scientific revolutions.

But Tyson sometimes offers another, more spontaneous, and perhaps more revealing motivation for the remake: the passage of time since Sagan's *Cosmos*. For example, in an interview at a Comic-Con comic book convention:

> Host: "Why are we rebooting *Cosmos*?"
> Tyson: "It's been 34 years!"

More elaborately, for a podcast interview with "The POD Delusion" in the UK:

> Host: "So why *Cosmos* and why now?"
> Tyson: "So, its been an entire generation, more than 30 years since the last *Cosmos* appeared, and it's high time that it returned in a way that can serve our next generation...."

This passage-of-time answer is intoned with assurance, as though everyone must be familiar with a constant of entropy in contemporary television culture. It seems that the cosmos$_1$ must be periodically regenerated even when our understanding of the cosmos$_2$ remains relatively stable.

In the mythoscientific makeover, is there anything like the Kuhnian phases of "normal science" and "crisis"? Vaguely there may be. "Normal science" might have as its mythoscientific equivalent something like "normal viewing"—a relatively uneventful phase in which network re-broadcasts, syndications, and DVD sales continue at a regular pace. A fall-off in these is the source of the "crisis," eventually necessitating a re-make. It's not that the scientific paradigm has come to be judged inadequate to handle the anomalies—it's just that nobody is watching.

The official trailer for Tyson's *Cosmos* is an intriguing document. Within the first few moments, one experiences the passage from normal viewing to crisis in the trailer's only two spoken segments, both voiceovers. The first is by Sagan, from the opening of the original *Cosmos* series; backed by a new-age styled serene ambient music, Sagan slowly and mellifluously says, "The cosmos is all that is, or ever was, or ever will be. Our contemplations of the cosmos stir us. We know we are approaching the grandest of mysteries." Then, with abrupt and resonant authority, Tyson breaks in with, "It's time to get going again." Thereupon follows a fast and furious parade of images and sounds, which, if encountering them unaware of their source, one might reasonably take to be a collage of cinematic and musical styles and effects for fantasy and science fiction fare of the last several decades—films like *Lord of the Rings*, *The Matrix*, and the more recent *Star Trek* series and films. The meager proportion of scientific proposition to image in the trailer confirms just what it is that has been remade.

The remake of Sagan is partly about ritually keeping him alive. In recent years Sagan has undergone an intriguing secular hagiographic process. Celebrated saints and holy people are typically inscribed into temporal periodicities of two kinds: those of set calendrical periods such as weeks, years, or millennia; and those keyed to the human life-cycle and typically geared toward recruitment into specific social statuses.

As I write this, we are nearing the seventh annual Carl Sagan day (November 9, Sagan's birthday), a festival promoted by the Committee for Skeptical Inquiry and other secularist and rationalist organizations, and accompanied by eating the ritual food of apple pie— made famous (eternalized?) by the opening proposition of the *Cosmos* episode "The Lives of the Stars": "If you wish to make an apple pie from scratch, you must first invent the universe."

The opening of Tyson's *Cosmos* series is much like the opening of the trailer mentioned above, except that Tyson's first words now are, "A generation ago, the astronomer Carl Sagan stood here and launched hundreds of millions of us on a great adventure." Aimed at recruitment for science, the generational theme adds a life-cycle periodicity to Sagan's life after death. A few moments further into *Cosmos*, Tyson voices the generational theme in a different way— specifically to introduce a litany of basic rules of the scientific method. The litany opens with, "This adventure is made possible by generations of searchers strictly adhering to a simple set of rules," and closes with, "Accept these terms and the cosmos is yours." The very appeal to generational kinship recalls Sagan, for whom cosmic kinship formed a recurrent literary trope: evolutionary kinship binds all life on earth, and ultimately we will fulfill our destiny to colonize the cosmos, binding it together through a cosmic diaspora with our "pale blue dot" as starting point and center. In such speculations Sagan plays to our geocentric impulses as well as to the grand, appealing image of cosmic kinship that appears repeatedly in world mythology (for example, in the form of Sky and Earth begetting the family of beings that make up the cosmos).

To the consternation of some scientists, Kuhn portrayed normal science and paradigm crisis as resulting in part from processes having less to do with the physical sciences than with sociology—specifically, with the maintenance and collapse of communities: "Like the choice between competing political institutions, that between competing paradigms proves to be a choice between incompatible modes of community life." There are important communal factors in the *Cosmos* remake as well, and the three principals in the *Cosmos* remake each passionately articulates a particular strand. Druyan discusses her desire to keep her late husband's dreams alive. Tyson often repeats a story about how Sagan took a special interest in him when he was about to begin graduate school, which left Tyson with a sense of responsibility towards Sagan's legacy; the story appears as a tribute to Sagan at the end of the first episode of the new *Cosmos*. MacFarlane, a science buff, tells of the importance of Sagan's *Cosmos* in his own youth and the need for a similar experience for today's young people.

The considerations above suggest parallels, but also something that has no equivalent in Kuhn's formulation: that in the realm of popular culture one can sometimes keep a product alive only by remaking it—that is by offering an established product freshened up. Vis-à-vis Kuhn, the relation of science and community is here largely reversed: in Kuhn's revolutions, new developments in science can break apart a scientific community, while in the case of *Cosmos*, it is as though periodic change is necessary to maintain a community. The purpose of the change is to realign pretty much the same science with a rapidly-changing mass-cultural aesthetic, specifically with the visual and aural styles and iconography to which viewers are continuously, willingly, and interactively retrained to respond—so that they will have an up-to-date cosmos$_2$, but more importantly a resonant, relevant, re-pixelated cosmos$_1$. If successful the new product will not only update but innovate in ways that leave competitors feeling the need to innovate. I will not attempt to characterize the differences in detail, but in the most general terms, Tyson's *Cosmos*, compared to Sagan's, is much slicker and faster-paced, with more elaborate animations and more sophisticated "effects." Tyson's music calls comparatively more toward action-adventure, Sagan's more towards contemplation. Sagan's *Cosmos*, which originally seemed lavish, now is spartan—a sort of *Watch Mr. Wizard* (for those who can still recall) compared to the later pizzazz of *Bill Nye the Science Guy*. All of this would seem symptomatic of a Lévi-Straussian "hot" society getting ever hotter.

Both Sagan's *Cosmos* and Tyson's *Cosmos* contain a greater variety of audio and visual styles than one could get away with in any other television series; surely this reflects viewers' readiness to allow greater latitude when the topic is cosmology$_1$—the great inventory, the totalizing fashion-statement. Temporally, science and mythoscience would seem to be pulling in opposite directions. According to contemporary science, the cosmos$_2$ may be in a state of expansion that will continue forever; while it would seem that we can now expect to get only about thirty-four years out of a mythoscientific cosmos$_1$—considerably less than the life-expectancy of the cosmos$_2$ though at least greater than that of clothing styles and many home appliances.

4
Raw and Cooked Redux

In recent decades the mythic story of the acquisition of cooking-fire as the origin of the human difference has come back around in the form of modern science. Here I will analyze one variant of the modern scientific cooking-fire myth, specifically the recent book *Cooked: A Natural History of Transformation* (2013) by prolific real-food writer Michael Pollan. I will then briefly relate the Pollan variant to three other modern scientific variants, each of which evokes a different aspect of what Claude Lévi-Strauss, in his now-classic work, has said about this scenario as it is recounted in archaic or traditional mythologies.

The aspect of Lévi-Strauss's theory that jumps out as immediately relevant to Pollan's *Cooked* is "The Science of the Concrete," the opening essay of *The Savage Mind*, in which Lévi-Strauss formulates a pivotal distinction between what he terms Neolithic Science and Modern Science. In *Cooked*, Pollan frequently mentions Lévi-Strauss's theories about culinary anthropology and the cooking-fire theme in mythology, but he neglects "The Science of the Concrete"—a circumstance perhaps related to the fact that this theme is most fully formulated by Lévi-Strauss not in his writings on myth *per se* but rather in his works on "savage" classification. Still, the Neolithic/Modern science distinction elaborated in "The Science of the Concrete" flows directly and seamlessly into Lévi-Strauss's theories of myth and culinary anthropology; and it is likely that Pollan's formulations in *Cooked* were at least indirectly influenced by the distinction.

What does Lévi-Strauss have in mind by Neolithic and Modern science? The distinction (between, hereafter, N-science and M-science) addresses the varying levels of organization at which humans have attempted to classify nature and make it amenable to human ends such as health and nutrition. N-science is adapted to "perception and the imagination" while M-science is "at a remove from it." N-science groups, analyzes, and manipulates the natural world at the level of the tastes, colors, and shapes we perceive without specialized technical apparatus. The M-science "remove" Lévi-Strauss has in mind we have already encountered in one variety, specifically in the concept of *atoms* which fall below the level of the senses and are only revealed through some combination of analytical reason, experimentation, and sometimes technical instrumentation. Partly to differentiate his view of N-science from earlier theories of savage "protoscience," Lévi-Strauss emphasizes that N-science is indeed a science: not an assemblage of ad hoc superstitions, but rather a robust, self-consistent, theoretical, and expandable system built up through history via astute observation of and interaction with nature.

Lévi-Strauss also elaborates the distinction between N- and M-science through a contrast between practitioners who epitomize the two: the practitioner of N-science is, metaphorically, a *bricoleur* or *handyman*; the practitioner of M-science is the *engineer*. The handyman works with a traditional set of tools (concepts), though sometimes achieving creative and unexpected results by devising new ways to use them (as well as the leftover odds-and-ends from his last project); the engineer, unsentimental about his tool kit, continually pushes to invent new tools (concepts) and leave the old ones behind. Particularly on the level of the practitioners and their attitudes Lévi-Strauss admits that the distinction is not absolute; as an approximation, the way of thinking about nature that brought us animal domestication and traditional breeding practices would seem to belong to N-science, while growth-hormones, antibiotics, and genetic engineering would belong to M-science.

It is clear that the distinction between M- and N-science and their respective practitioners correlates with yet another distinction important to Lévi-Strauss, although this one he elaborates not in the opening but rather in the concluding essays of *The Savage Mind*. The contrast is between two worldviews: one belonging to "cold" societies, those whose energies go into preserving a given ideal, the other to "hot" societies, or those that have given up the idea of societal continuity of design in favor of a series of non-repeating changes. Here too the contrast Lévi-Strauss offers is more ideal-type than absolute. The cold-hot contrast originally generated considerable misunderstanding, including the charge that Lévi-Strauss was claiming that "cold" societies were changeless and had no history. The criticism was misdirected; all societies, Lévi-Strauss accepts, have change and history. The contrast is, rather, between ideals: some societies are committed to preserving continuity in so far as possible, while others choose to revel in the lack of it. The contrast amounts to the attitudes of the handyman and the engineer generalized as worldviews; or conversely, the handyman and engineer are "cold" vs. "hot" inflected at the level of individual practice.

Finally, Lévi-Strauss also compares N- and M-science in terms of their efficacy: bluntly, which is better? Lévi-Strauss is clear that the findings of neither N- nor M-science are entirely right or wrong. His overriding point is that from the standpoint of M-science the intellectual sophistication and efficacy of N-science has been consistently underestimated—a misjudgment patent in the relegation of N-science practice to the realm of "magic" (though, by a rhetorical quirk, Pollan and other food writers revel in that term). Yet in different respects Lévi-Strauss himself favors one or the other. From the standpoint of pragmatically describing the workings of nature, Lévi-Strauss sometimes favors M-science by, in effect, admitting that M-science can reveal real processes not detectable by the unaided senses. Also, Lévi-Strauss describes the successes of N-science through the perspective of M-science (and not the other way around) as though the approach of the latter is broader and encompasses the former. For example, he notes that "On intuitive grounds alone we might group onions, garlic, cabbage, turnips, radishes and mustard together.... In confirmation of the evidence of the senses, chemistry shows that these different families are united on another plane: they contain sulphur."

Aesthetically, however, Lévi-Strauss favors N-science, where nature is envisioned through principles of interconnection and order that also provide artistic satisfaction. Regarding the two sciences, Lévi-Strauss's attitude might be described as the disappointment of a medieval philosopher upon discovering that the transcendentals of the true and the beautiful only partially converge. And particularly when one considers "the science of the concrete" in the context of Lévi-Strauss's larger defense of "savage" thought and society, it is clear that there is also a supervening moral context in which Lévi-Strauss favors N-science, namely, the claim that it supports a way of life more geared to harmony than to exploitive destruction of the natural world.

Neo-Neolithic Science?

There is little in *Cooked* to suggest that Pollan is directly conversant with Lévi-Strauss's distinction between Neolithic and Modern science specifically, and Pollan does not use these terms. Yet regarding all four contrasts just discussed—the level or organization at which nature is engaged, the attitudes of the practitioner, the surrounding worldview, and the relative efficacy of the two sciences—there are clear affinities between Pollan's *Cooked* and Lévi-Strauss's "The Science of the Concrete": both works are valorizations of (using Levi-Strauss's terms) Neolithic science in a world given over to Modern science.

For Lévi-Strauss N-science begins in classification. For *Cooked*, Pollan devises a four-fold classification of cooking methods, which simultaneously forms the book's macro-organization. The four forms of cooking correspond to the ancient four-element theory: grilling (fire), boiling (water), baking (air), and the cold-cooking of fermentation (the microbial earth).

The choice of the four elements is itself telling, since the theory derives from the era of the so-called Greek miracle, in which we find many formulations among early pre-Socratic philosophers that defy classification as either mythology or science. The theory gives us a world of "elements" rather than gods, but they are the elements towards which the personifying mind first turns, and they lie at the level of everyday perception, prior to any analytical decomposition. The four-element theory might be described as N-science's finest hour or (with atomism already looming in the pre-Socratic era) its last stand, but Pollan prefers thinking of it as in some sense eternal.

> The fact that modern science has dismissed the classical elements, reducing them to still more elemental substances and forces—water to molecules of hydrogen and oxygen; fire to a process of rapid oxidation, etc.—hasn't really changed our lived experience of nature or the way we imagine it. Science may have replaced the big four with a periodic table of 118 elements, and then reduced each of those to even-tinier particles, but our senses and our dreams have yet to get the news.

Dissatisfaction with M-science registers with particular intensity in Pollan's recoil from engineered food, which he sees as a creation of the "reductive lens of Western science" applied to modern food production. Pollan's book is full of examples—from modern, engineered pork (a "creation of science, industry, and inhumanity") to the processes used in the production of the iconic Wonder Bread. A recurrent theme is that gains in efficiency of production in modern food processing have often led to declines in nutritional value and health benefits, seemingly because the analytical units that have been identified miss something—perhaps "synergies" between components or some "X-factor" that science has failed to identify, or, more philosophically, "that a whole food might actually be more than the sum of its nutrient parts."

Besides the rejection of the engineering stance toward food occasioned by its negative consequences, there is also a more positive side to Pollan's advocacy of the N-science approach to food. In this more positive vein there are two recurrent positive themes, and both correspond to characteristics of N-science for which Lévi-Strauss adjudged it preferable to M-Science. One of these (already implied in the passage quoted above) is aesthetic merit, for *Cooked* is full of appeals to sensory pleasure, especially with respect to smell, a sense from which we humans have become alienated and need to recapture. Pollan's sensual characterizations frequently pull us into the metaphysical, as in this mythological allusion:

> the *idea* of meat, the smoky, ethereal trace of animal flesh wafting up to heaven, is what the gods want from us.... The fragrant column of smoke, symbolizing the link between heaven and earth, is the only conceivable medium of conveyance, and also communication, between humans and their gods. So to say this aroma is divine is more than an empty expression.

The other positive theme is durability, and there is at least a degree of overlap between the ideal that Lévi-Strauss termed "cold" and the one that Pollan and others of the present moment summarize as "sustainable." The subtitle of Pollan's book is *A Natural History of Transformation*, which might suggest both a notion of human history and a human engagement of nature through transformations that are already given in nature as humans find it—as opposed to forms of transformation induced by engineers.

It should not be concluded that the pull-back to N-science by Pollan implies a rejection of M-science. His criticism seems to be not so much that M-science is false as that it is incomplete and inadequate to the complexity of food. There is also a sense that for human endeavors closely related to sensory aesthetics N-science will always remain paramount. There is a great deal of M-science in *Cooked*, and it is brought in for two main purposes, both serving to confirm the reliability of N-science. One purpose is to inform and amaze us by revealing what is going on below the surface, but in a way that confirms what we already had figured out intuitively or through trial and error—in much the manner described by Lévi-Strauss above. Consider the following passage:

> Corn kernels, like the seeds of many other grasses, contain plenty of sugars, but they are not in a form that *S. cerevisiae* can make use of. The sugars are tightly bound together in long carbohydrate chains that the tiny yeasts can't break apart.... But certain enzymes can cleave those carbohydrate chains into simple, fermentable sugars, and, as the earliest beer makers discovered, one of those enzymes—ptyalin—is present in human saliva.... To this day, there are indigenous groups in South America that rely on the chewing method to make an alcoholic beverage called chicha—a corn-and-saliva beer.

The other purpose for M-science in *Cooked* rests on an implicit acknowledgement of the capacity of M-Science for self-correction: if M-science has failed to engineer healthy food, it has succeeded, in some cases at least, in explaining its engineering failures—often with the injunction that we should consider putting things back the way they were. This theme is particularly strong in the fermentation section, which considers a number of emerging M-science theories about possible harmful consequences of our anti-microbial and possibly overly-hygienic ethos. In sum, the role of M-science in *Cooked* is mostly confirmatory: N-science should make food judgments, and M-science should confirm them.

Yet despite these correspondences, Pollan's N-science in the end has only a partial overlap with the N-science Lévi-Strauss writes about. The bulk of *Cooked* is organized around a series of journeys in which Pollan seeks out and visits food people who, by circumstance or choice, have had limited connection to the corporate food industry. He attempts to recover techniques that have remained largely unchanged over the centuries, beginning with a trip to the Carolinas in search of a primal experience of pit-roasted meat. And perhaps his salvage operation succeeds to an extent—as much as it is possible to recover archaic gastronomy in the contemporary US. But in contrast to the systems of indigenous science that Lévi-Strauss describes, Pollan's perspective came into being as a conscious, mid-life, literary construction pulled together from academic and field research and other sources for the purposes of a book—rather than as an organized system of knowledge whose tradition he inherited. Not even the practice of cooking, let alone its science, came to Pollan to any great extent from lived tradition, since in the family in which he was raised it was done by his mother. *Cooked* is partly about Pollan's learning to cook, and he concludes by offering one recipe for each of the classical elements, from the pastiche of archaic culinary practices he has discovered on the road.

As noted above, N-science, in Lévi-Strauss's view, is the level at which traditional origin myths are formulated. Myths are N-science narrativized: stories that enlist sensorily registered distinctions such as raw and cooked or fresh and rotten to advance foundational sociological and cosmological truths. Pollan's N-science does incorporate a number of narratives, for *Cooked* is full of stories, organized under the four elements, about his encounters with various food-people from the barbecue pit-master (fire) to a raw-cheese making nun (earth) who brings to her craft a religio-metaphysical flare that equals Pollan's (above) on divine smoke. These stories offer a "mythology" in the broad, popular-culture sense of the term: they take our pulse and serve to epitomize and energize important currents in our present-day self-conception. But despite the metaphysical exegeses offered by particular individuals, such stories are just not the sort of socio-cosmically founding narratives that Lévi-Strauss deals with in his work on mythology. Indeed, from a Lévi-Straussian perspective the most interesting quirk about Pollan's book is that Pollan has reinvented N-science without simultaneously reinventing its narrative expansion into an origin myth. The disconnection bespeaks another way in which Pollan's N-science is literarily constructed, partial, and compartmentalized vis-à-vis the N-science described by Lévi-Strauss. The reasons for Pollan's premature curtailment of N-science will become clear shortly.

A stop-over on a return journey never lands one in the same spot as that occupied by the traveler who, on the same journey, has not yet reached the turn-around point. Pollan's post-Pasteurian protest "on behalf of the senses and the microbes" would not be necessary in the world before M-science, but neither would it be possible before M-science definitively revealed these entities to us. A similar situation is faced in all our present post-isms. But even here Pollan is consistent with Lévi-Strauss—not so much with the peoples to whom Lévi-Strauss attributes N-science, but with the situation Pollan and Lévi-Strauss share as modern academics. It is notable that most of Lévi-Strauss's techniques and metaphors (optics, modern astronomy and space-travel, Boolean algebra, etc.) are drawn from the world of M-science—giving his theories modern authority. And Pollan's pull-back is only partial (more on this below). Artful primitivism has always been a constitutive component of the modern. The situation is rife with potential for self-indulgence and disingenuousness, but neither Lévi-Strauss nor Pollan is entirely naïve about such things. In an M-science world, the role of N-science, whether as an object of historic/ethnographic theorizing by Lévi-Strauss or a practical reconstruction for the kitchen by Pollan, would seem to be socio-political critique and moral reform via an appeal to the wisdom or imagined wisdom of other times and places.

Pollan's Origin Myth

But here's the thing: when it comes to our *origin myth*, what we encounter in Pollan is not a pull-back to N-science, but the opposite: enthrallment with the possibility of transcending our N-science myths of origin (Prometheus and the other traditional cooking-fire myths of the world) with an M-science bio-evolutionary scenario that delivers the same message, only, he believes, more powerfully. M-science triumphant over N-science. The particular M-science origin myth that Pollan advocates, adopting it as his own, is the "cooking hypothesis" proposed by Harvard bio-anthropologist Richard Wrangham, most popularly in his 2009 book, *Catching Fire: How Cooking Made Us Human.* Wrangham claims that, by breaking down food in advance, cooking allowed our evolutionary ancestors to, in Pollan's summation, trade "a big gut for a big brain," thus allowing the emergence of our predecessor *Homo erectus.*

Evolutionary science has become progressively and explicitly "M-" in orientation as the fossil record has come to be examined increasingly from the standpoint of the chemistry of evolution, including processes of nutrition and digestion. And one is forced to ask whether there is presently any M-science more complex and incomplete—and more inviting of premature, speculative, and partisan origin scenarios—than human evolutionary biology, with its vast geographic and chronological gaps, and its trail of discarded hypotheses and contenders for the *human difference.* On this topic the intrafamilial squabbles of evolutionists can approach the intensity of their battles with creationists. Pollan is aware of the legacy of controversy and admits that so far "Wrangham's most convincing arguments are deductive," but he is aglow with confidence in this hypothesis' explanatory power and chance for success. Nowhere in Pollan's commentary is there even a hint that the incompleteness of bio-evolutionary M-science should lead us to pull back from Wrangham's cooking hypothesis specifically or, more generally, from our seeming need for an origin myth. Over against those who would "dismiss it as another 'just so' story," he asks:

But, really, how much more can we expect when trying to account for something like the advent of ourselves? What the cooking hypothesis gives us is a compelling modern myth—one cast in the language of evolutionary biology rather than religion—locating the origins of our species in the discovery of cooking with fire. To call it a myth is not to belittle it. Like any other such story, it serves to explain how what is came to be using the most powerful vocabulary available, which in our case today happens to be that of evolutionary biology.

What does "most powerful vocabulary" mean? Most accurate? Most persuasive? Most prestigious? Pollan follows this comment, and concludes his main discussion of Wrangham's cooking hypothesis, by noting that both classical mythology and bio-evolutionary theory now have located the origins of our humanity in the cooking fire, and he suggests that "that coincidence is all the confirmation we can hope for." Considering that it follows upon his lengthy exposition of the merits of Wrangham's M-science cooking hypothesis, Pollan's comment is, in a sense, a generous gesture towards the traditional mythology of fire—the mythology that arose in the N-science epoch. Yet the comment betokens a use of N-science—bringing it in after M-science, for confirmation—that reverses the relation found in the rest of his book, where, as we've seen, N-science is the beacon and it is M-science that serves to confirm. In *Cooked* there is thus a reversal of hierarchy in the methodology for assessing what we should *eat* vs. what we *are*: in the kitchen and farm, a pull-back to N-science as highest authority, and for our origin myth a push-forward to M-science as highest authority. (Or the phrasing could be reversed: a push-forward to the neo-N-science for the aware consumer vs. a pull-back, or fall back, for our origin myth, to the default position of our era, at least for most academics, i.e., the dominance of M-science.) The power of M-science in contemporary consciousness is nowhere more powerfully illustrated than when Pollan nudges us, in accounting for our origin, to opt for the M-science approach to nutrition even in this book about the ill effects of our having once done so.

Why the shift? Pollan does not comment on the matter, so I speculate. One obvious difference is that origin myths would fall in the category of *theory* while cooking is *applied*; the risk of negative consequences flowing from mistakes of course looms with greater immediacy in applied than in theoretical science. Incomplete science—science prematurely applied—in the kitchen can kill you; it actually is killing us, Pollan and others argue, through the various metabolic disorders now epidemic in the modern world. Although as the history of warfare shows, your origin myth can get you killed too, in the context in which Pollan is writing the likelihood is not immanent—removing, or at least lessening, one of the possible penalties of embracing a theory that is plausible and appealing but incomplete and unproven.

The nutrition science from which Pollan now recoils arrived in mid-twentieth century amidst fanfare and high seriousness at least equal to that with which Wrangham's cooking hypothesis has now been launched. Pollan's readiness to give the benefit of the doubt to the latter, even while protesting the former, may be related not so much to the *evidence for* as to the *message of* the cooking hypothesis. The message is right, for the cooking hypothesis supports—using evolutionary biology, "the most powerful vocabulary available"—the moral vision to which Pollan and his book lend support: the centrality of cooking in human well-being. The energy that Pollan directs towards connecting cooking with well-being is striking: the benefits will be physical, moral, and cultural, and will emerge at multiple levels—personal, interpersonal, familial, and socio-political. Indeed, the loss of community reappears as a constitutive defect of Western reductive science, i.e., that it "has always been better at understanding individuals (pathogens, variables, elements, whatever) than communities." One of the more intimate social benefits forms a leitmotif in Pollan's travel narratives, specifically his sharing of his experiments with members of his immediate family and especially his son Isaac. This motif—not to mention asides by Pollan about the increasing Zen-quotient in his cooking—recalls another modestly countercultural best-seller from a different generation, Robert Pirsig's 1974 work, *Zen and the Art of Motorcycle Maintenance*. Although the final products diverge somewhat, these two books, Pollan's and Pirsig's, are built by intermixing the same ingredients: "on the road" in America; father-son bonding; readiness to make mid-course life-adjustments; the romance of reclaiming archaic, exotic wisdom (which invariably turns out to be more holistic than our present-day regimen); and all these—indeed human well-being generally—condensed, metaphorically and metonymically, into acquiring hands-on self-reliance, whether learning to cook or to tune one's own motorcycle.

In most cases we do not exactly know how a given origin myth was created, but here is a good guess: through projection into the past, *as our moment of origin*, and in the strongest form of expression available, of whatever the mythmaker thinks should be the ruling moral vision of the present. Pollan is talking about one myth, but his comment about the new scientific version of the origin of humanity through cooking-fire, and its greater power in our time than the old, traditional myths such as Prometheus, resonates with a theme encountered often in contemporary popular science writing: the idea that, in biologist E.O. Wilson's words, science is giving rise to a "new mythos" of surpassing power: "Material reality discovered by science already possesses more content and grandeur than all religious cosmologies combined." What happens to archaic myths (those that arose from N-science) in the world of M-science? The answer is the same for Pollan, Wilson, and many others in our era: archaic mythologies, shorn of religious and/or ritual contexts, are re-purposed as sources of psychological and sociological insight and as backup support for M-science claims—whether in the form of convergent findings, useful metaphors, or just a bit of added poetic flare.

In the end Pollan leaves us with a multi-stranded temporal perspective which involves both bio-evolutionary process and human culture. There is, first of all, the great bio-evolutionary transformation which gave rise to the animal that does something no other animal does—cooks—and from that moment onward cooking is our fate; we can no longer survive without it. While Pollan acknowledges that our eating habits have induced some changes to ourselves and other species, the nutritional situation since the great transformation, if not entirely static, has been...let's say the bio-evolutionary expression of the Slow Food movement. For our food choices we should rely on two factors: our biologically inherited sense of taste, evolutionarily-honed to distinguish between the nutritious and the noxious (though it can be manipulated and misled by clever M-science); and on the cuisines of the world—the array of food traditions built up over time through trial and error.

Pollan presents the communal cooked meal as a sort of necessity and a given of human social life, one which our society has managed to slip away from, but at the same time he argues that its social construction can and should be modified in progressive ways, most notably in removing the unfair burden the cooked communal meal has often put on women. But if the organization of the communal meal should be modified, the socially progressive thing to do regarding the actual content and methods of cooking is to mostly go back to the way food was before M-science took control of it. Vis-à-vis Lévi-Strauss's distinction between "cold" and "hot" societies, there are both similarities and differences in Pollan's perspective. Pollan's view of the guiding light offered by the world cuisines might be described, from a Lévi-Straussian perspective, as the best of N-science: these cuisines offer a rigorous, empirically-grounded, robust accumulation of beneficial and aesthetically pleasing knowledge and practice formulated over a long period of time prior to the M-science era. In Lévi-Strauss's view, "hot" vs. "cold" attitudes toward time form a matter of cultural choice: a society commits to keeping things the way they were, or to constant turnover, or to some place in between. Pollan's approach to food and cooking would thus be in Lévi-Strauss's (perhaps unfortunate) terms "cold," while his approach to reforming the social organization of cooking and the epistemology of our origin myth would be "hot." But Pollan's assessment incorporates a biological component missing in Levi-Strauss's distinction. While

Pollan would seem to think that we are malleable, or biologically unconstrained, in such matters as division of labor by gender for cooking, so that these can be reformed, we are biologically constrained in terms of *what* we should cook and eat, and we should make the cultural choice to recognize as much. For reasons that are ultimately biological, M-science has failed on the level of nutrition; Pollan's discussion of "molecular gastronomy"—or M-science in the interests of taste— draws heavily on the view of chef Bittor Arguinzoniz, who leaves the impression that, for the hubris it displays in the face of our genes, this movement too is doomed to fail.

Four Modern Scientific Fire Myths

Pollan's is the fourth scientific fire-myth variant that I have analyzed, and in each case a different aspect of Lévi-Strauss's perspective on myth furnishes a fruitful take-off point. The bio-evolutionary theory set forth by Richard Wrangham in his *Catching Fire*—the scenario that Pollan incorporates as his origin myth—is the variant most readily related to Lévi-Strauss's perspective, for Wrangham largely accepts Lévi-Strauss's summary of the place of fire in human culture as it is recounted in mythologies: cooking-fire ushers in a cluster of cultural innovations that include new technologies and forms of social organization and socio-political alliance. But while Lévi-Strauss approaches the scenario as offering symbolic ruminations on the nature of society and human existence, Wrangham approaches the origin of cooking as an actual event, one with major bio-evolutionary consequences: it was the critical factor in the emergence of *Homo erectus*, precursor of *Homo sapiens*. Another modern fire myth, created a few decades earlier, was J.J. Annaud's popular film, *Quest for Fire* (*La Guerre du Feu*, 1981). Annaud casts the story of the acquisition of fire-making as a cinematic epic rather than a cinematic myth. I argue that despite the increased naturalism of the epic genre—a commitment that seemingly would make it more suitable than myth for science exposition—the choice of epic for topics that for us are cosmically-defining leads to degradation in narrative power, as Lévi-Strauss has demonstrated in Native American oral narrative. And in Pollan's neo-Neolithic science, as discussed above, we seem to have the reemergence of the pivotal contrast drawn by Lévi-Strauss in "The Science of the Concrete."

A fourth variant, and the most complex, is offered by Cambridge astronomer John D. Barrow in his *The Artful Universe* (1995, 2005). This work proffers what has come to be termed a "Goldilocks" view of the cosmos, one which emphasizes the range of physical conditions on earth whose values are not too large, and not too small, but just right for supporting human life and culture. In the midst of his presentation Barrow tries to show that the fire-domesticator, whom he regards also as the culture-initiator, would have to be, among other requirements, a being of approximately human size; the condition is summarized in the "nice coincidence that coal, wood, or peat fires have to be of a minimum size in order to maintain the ignition temperature of the ingredients under typical atmospheric conditions; and that minimum size is just about what is required to keep a human being warm in a natural shelter of convenient size." Thus, at the center of Barrow's Goldilocks cosmos sits a Goldilocks fire-myth. As part of his demonstration, Barrow shows how alternative fire-makers would have failed; but the alternatives he defeats are invariably anthropocentrically imagined. For example, he shows that a miniature human could not have domesticated fire, but he neglects to consider what a smaller being of *alternative design* might have accomplished if cosmic evolution, which Barrow admits is full of contingent events, had gone another way. Barrow's analysis, in other words, is stacked from the start. The flaws offer new scientific variations, conveyed through impressive-looking quantitative measures and charts, on the tenacious anthropocentrism that Lévi-Strauss has emphasized through his work on traditional cooking-fire myths. Three of these authors—Wrangham, Pollan, and Annaud—make strong appeals to the social, often in the form of kinship, and in this general way the new variants are consonant with the traditional mythology of cooking-fire. The exception is Barrow, whose lone fire-maker in a studio-cave offers an archaically inflected image of individualism, and in this sense is the most modern of the four.

I regard my analyses of the four variants as a tribute to Lévi-Strauss, attested in part by the continued applicability of his theories in the "post-mythological" world, the world of modern science—as though not much has happened, or, alternatively, as though Lévi-Strauss's perspective anticipated the possible further developments. It is a nice coincidence that Pollan hit on the *four* elements, since fours run through Lévi-Strauss, from the four volumes of the *Mythologiques* to the four relations comprised in the atom of kinship (*The Elementary Structures of Kinship*)—perhaps reflecting, in turn, the patterns of four that run through Native American mythology, Lévi-Strauss's greatest scholarly forte. Parenthetically and in the interests of the post-cooking cleanup, I speculate that theorist of modern myth extraordinaire Roland Barthes, who excels at finding the archaic in the modern, is also alluding to the four-element theory in his vignette "Soap-powders and Detergents" (from his *Mythologies*). Specifically, Barthes classifies advertisements for modern cleaning agents into three kinds: those that appeal to their powers of solubility (water), foaming action (air), and abrasion (which, he claims, invariably evokes the image of fire—think Comet cleanser). That leaves earth, inflected as "dirt," expressing the need for cleaning.

On the Genesis of Modern Mythology

Besides the "science of the concrete," there is one other way in which Pollan's variant marks something new vis-à-vis the other three variants just mentioned—though this is a point long familiar, and perhaps mainly of interest, to a mythologist. Assuming that Pollan's reading of Lévi-Strauss played some role in the shaping of *Cooked*, Pollan's work becomes another instance of an increasingly common pattern in which mythic structures that have been abstracted by scholars in the study of traditional mythologies are turned around and used as blueprints or "generative grammars" for creating new myths for the world of contemporary popular culture. This seems to be especially common for myth or folk narrative analyses that have a linear diagrammatic character, the most familiar examples being Vladimir Propp's *The Morphology of the Folktale* and Joseph Campbell's *The Hero With A Thousand Faces*, the latter of which George Lucas readily cites as providing the blueprint for the *Star Wars* films. Campbell and

Propp sit ready on the shelves of screenwriters, but their influence is not limited to Hollywood. For example, in the book quoted above, E.O. Wilson says in a footnote that he learned how to mythologize the story of science from Joseph Campbell and a screenwriter's manual that it had spawned. And Wilson is not the only science popularizer to acknowledge Campbell.

The connection of scholarly and popular culture with respect to the cooking-fire myth was already prepared by Wrangham, who opens his book by challenging the assumptions of the recent "raw food" movement, and in the meantime the Paleo Diet has appeared on the cultural scene. But in terms of popular cultural influence, Lévi-Strauss, at least until now, has fallen far short of either Propp or Campbell. The reason may rest partly with the difficulty of Lévi-Strauss's prose, but probably even more so with the kind of diagrams that Lévi-Strauss offers. In their own versions of modern analytical reductionism, both Campbell and Propp draw linear or "syntagmatic" diagrams of traditional mythic or folktale stories; for example, Campbell schematizes the first steps of the hero's journey as the call to adventure, refusal of the call, supernatural aid, and the crossing of the first threshold. Campbell's full list of steps amounts to a generalized and generalizable plot, and both Propp and Campbell also illustrate ways in which such chains can be tweaked to form new variations on a theme.

By contrast Lévi-Strauss operates at a still further remove (the quarks below the atoms?), offering diagrams not of plots but of deep, unresolvable polarities or conflicts (his so-called "binary oppositions") from which, he theorizes, plots arise. In most cases, such "paradigmatic" diagrams are of less immediate use to popular-culture creators who, above all, are charged with producing story plots. Pollan's project is an exception because, with his travel anecdotes for little stories and Wrangham's "cooking hypothesis" for his grand story, the real need, lying in the reverse direction, is for a generative opposition in which to frame all this. Lévi-Strauss's great distinction between Neolithic and Modern science, implicit in all his work on myth, also describes, approximately at least, the energizing tension underlying Pollan's *Cooked*, and given Pollan's familiarity with Lévi-Strauss it is likely that the distinction at some level contributed to Pollan's framing of his argument. To the extent that the latter is the case, Lévi-Strauss joins Campbell and Propp at the point at which scholarly analytical works about traditional mythology become an avenue for the creation of modern mythology. Such works become how-to manuals—cookbooks if you will—for serving up "new" mythologies in the popular sphere.

Science Saves Myth, Myth Saves Science

In my opening discussion I cited a title, one with an embedded proposition, by classicist Luc Brisson: *How Philosophers Saved Myths*. Brisson refers to the fact that, for love of myth, its very detractors found ways to save it through allegorical readings. The great tension between myth and philosophy in the classical and medieval worlds has since been replaced by the new tension between myth and science. But recast for the new situation, Brisson's proposition remains true: science, in the four scenarios I have just considered, saves myth. Gladwell draws on contemporary science to reinterpret the story of David and Goliath, giving it a contemporary relevance generalizable to situations that all of us face and independent of religious belief. Citing Epicurus' new science as making possible the Renaissance, Greenblatt revives the ancient champion of Epicureanism, Lucretius, who found a new use for the mythological gods and epic stories that the doctrine of materialism displaced: they became vehicles for enticing converts into the new worldview through poetic art. Admitting that "our doctrine often seems unpalatable," Lucretius bares his strategy: "That is why I have tried to administer my philosophy to you in the dulcet strains of poesy, to touch it with the sweet honey of the Muses." In the case of *Cosmos* and its remake, it is not particular myths that Sagan and Tyson are saving, but something more abstract: the spirit of mythology—the possibility of approaching the cosmos as a place of wonder and adventure with lessons to teach us. Pollan champions a modern bio-evolutionary origin myth, stressing its convergence with archaic mythologies and poetically sprinkling mythological allusions through his analysis. More importantly, he enlists modern science to confirm what Lévi-Strauss called Neolithic science but which James Frazer and others call magic or myth. Pollan rests authority more with the latter than with modern science, at least for decisions about food.

But even if Brisson's proposition, recast for science, remains true, it would not take much in the way of mental gymnastics to read the relations just described inversely: it is, rather, that myth is saving science. Were it not for the adventure, the narrative emplotment, and the resonant symbols, the scientific content in the cases just considered would implode from the public sphere into a black hole of specialized knowledge from which, due to conditions of extreme density, no enlightenment could escape. Or at least such a concern is recurrently voiced by many of the creators of contemporary myth-science mixtures. *Cosmos* and its remake are of special interest in this regard; they are part of a response to a peril perceived by Sagan and inherited by Tyson, one illustrated with melodramatic abandon in Sagan's millennium book, *The Demon-Haunted World: Science as a Candle in the Dark* (1996). In this book Sagan describes his personal terror that under the influence of pseudo-science the modern world is about to relapse into medieval darkness. The dichotomy of worldviews depicted by Sagan is not entirely unlike that portrayed by Greenblatt in *The Swerve*. With lurid orange and black cover and millennialist rhetoric, *Demon* displays the same strategy as we find in Lucretius: conjure a sense of danger and offer moral uplift and a way out— artfully peopling the remedy with heroes, villains, and the sense of adventure. In sum, in the contemporary popular world myth and science often fall into a rela-tionship of interdependence that is less dialectical than complementary or even co-evolutionary—each serv-ing to support and fill in where its companion epis-teme comes up short.

But we must not lose sight of the complexities; consider merely the more obvious ones created in the mixtures considered above. Gladwell offers a new metaphysics for an ancient story, without explicitly denying the old metaphysics; where does that leave us? Greenblatt is a humanistic scholar who, on one hand, credits a revised understanding of the physical world with the great, mythic transformation in human life, while, on the other, crediting a new artistic vision with engendering the spirit of science. It is not uncommon to hear that scientific progress propelled the remake of the television series *Cosmos*, but what is it that has really "progressed"—science or the popular aesthetics of television? Pollan engages two forms of science— one with affinities to traditional myth—in such a way as to create an epistemological disconnection between his advice for practical life and his vision of how we ultimately came to be. For the time being at least, it seems that our tale ends less in blissful, luminous synergy than in a situation rife with ambiguous and ambivalent authority. ■

Acknowledgements

I am grateful to Marshall Sahlins and Matthew Engelke of Prickly Paradigm Press for their encouragement and many helpful suggestions. For valuable and varied contributions I also thank my wife Cornelia Fales, Brandon Barker, Bill Hansen, Tom Mould, Daniel Peretti, and Bill Schrempp.

Also available from Prickly Paradigm Press:

continued

continued